Dinosaur Coloring Book For Kids and Toddlers

by Robert B. Grand

Dinosaur Coloring Book For Kids and Toddlers

With fun Dinosaur Facts for Kids

Copyright (c) 2018 Robert B. Grand

All rights reserved.
No part of this publication or the information in it may be quoted from or reproduced in any form by means such as printing, scanning, photocopying or otherwise without prior written permission of the copyright holder.
Cover design by germancreative.
Cover illustration: depositphotos.com

Printed in the USA

This Coloring Book Belongs to:

_____

_____

Did you know?

Dinosaurs were reptiles that lived on Earth from about 230 million years ago to about 65 million years ago.

Did you know?

The word "dinosaur"
was coined by British paleontologist
Richard Owen in 1842.
It is meaning "terrible lizard."

Did you know?

The first dinosaurs that appeared during the Triassic Period 230 million years ago were small and lightweight.

Did you know?

Scientists estimate that there were over 1,000 different species of non-avian dinosaurs and over 500 distinct genera. They speculate there are many still undiscovered dinosaurs and that there may be as many as 1,850 genera.

Did you know?

Snakes and lizards shed their skin when they grow. Researchers believe that dinosaurs may have done the same.

Did you know?

Some dinosaurs may have had colorful skin, but scientists don't know for sure. It's likely that most dinosaurs had green and brown scales to help them hide among trees and plants.

Did you know?

Like birds and reptiles today, dinosaurs built nests. Some even fed and protected their babies.

Did you know?

The first known American dinosaur was discovered in 1858 in the marl pits in Haddonfield, New Jersey.

Did you know?

The fastest dinosaur was the Ornithomimus.
It could run up to 43 mph.

Did you know?

Most dinosaurs were vegetarians.

Did you know?

Paleontologists find a fossil of a nonflying dinosaur that had feathers on its body.

Did you know?

Tyrannosaurus rex ate up to 22 tons of meat a year.

Did you know?

The longest dinosaur tooth ever recorded belonged to a T - Rex, and they were a 12 inches long.

Did you know?

A person who studies dinosaurs is known as a paleontologist.

Did you know?

Rather than being carnivores (meat eaters), the largest dinosaurs such as the Brachiosaurus and Apatosaurus were actually herbivores (plant eaters).

Did you know?

The Pentaceratops had the biggest skull at 10 feet long.

Did you know?

Dinosaurs lived within the Mesozoic Era, which included the Triassic, Jurassic, and Cretaceous periods, beginning 252 million years ago and ending 66 million years ago.

Did you know?

The toothiest dinosaur was the Hadrosaurs. It could have over 1,000 teeth and it continually grew new ones.

Did you know?

Many dinosaurs, like the massive predator know as Cryolophosaurus, were so equipped for the cold that they were able to live in Antarctica.

Did you know?

A T-Rex bite
was more than twice
as powerful as a lion bite.

Did you know?

The biggest dinosaur we currently know about is the Argentinosaurus. Paleontologists estimate it weighed up to 100 tons and measured 120 feet long.

Did you know?

Some pterosaurs had fur on their bodies to keep them warm.

Did you know?

Dinosaurs that could run on two legs were called bipeds.

Did you know?

The Megalodon was the biggest prehistoric fish. It looked like a shark, though it was three times bigger.

Did you know?

The asteroid that is believed to have wiped the dinosaurs out most likely struck Mexico's Yuctan Peninsula.

Did you know?

The Microraptor may be the smallest dinosaur ever.
It was only about 16 inches long, about the size of a pigeon.

Did you know?

One of the most intelligent dinosaurs was Troodon.

Did you know?

All dinosaurs laid eggs.
About 40 kinds of dinosaur eggs have been discovered.

Did you know?

Dinosaurs that lived near water often left the best fossils.

Did you know?

The name "Velociraptor" means speedy thief.

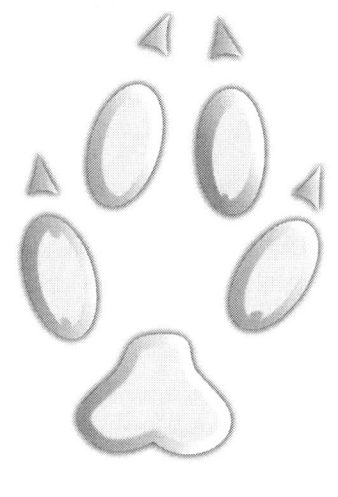 

Second set

If your kids have enjoyed this book, please consider leaving a short review on the books Amazon page. It will help the others to make an informed decision before buying my book.

Thank you so much.

Made in the USA
San Bernardino,
CA

"REVELATION"

TRIUMPH ENTERTAINMENT
Division of Triumph Books
601 South LaSalle Street
Chicago, Illinois 60605

©2000 Contents H&S Media, Inc.
All rights reserved.

Editor: John Delavan

Contributors:
Erin Brereton
David Fantle
Amy Helmes
Thomas Johnson
Geri Sahn

Design: Kai's Kreations, Inc.

This publication is not sponsored or endorsed by 98B or anyone affiliated with the group or its management.

98° CONTENTS

Back In Business	4
Pinups	8
98° Biography: Justin Jeffre	16
98° Biography: Drew Lachey	26
98° Biography: Nick Lachey	36
98° Biography: Jeff Timmons	46
98° Turns up the Heat	56
They Said It!	64
98° Live	66
Sites for Sore Eyes	74
Pinups	78
Fifty Fast Facts	80
98° Discography	84
Test Your 98° I.Q.	86
Caught on Film	92

This publication is not sponsored or endorsed by 98ß or anyone affiliated with the group or its management.

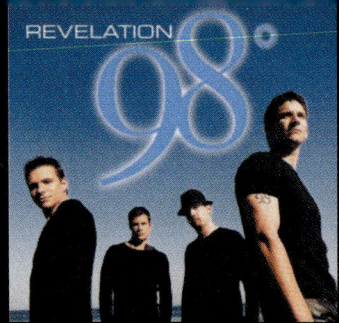

BACK IN BUSINESS

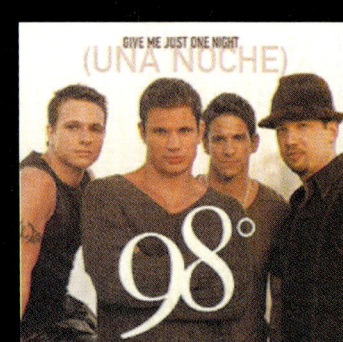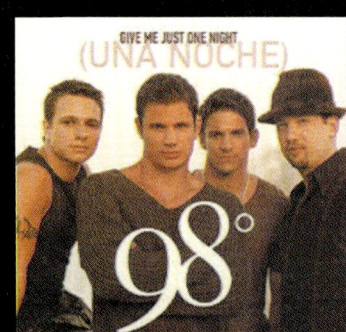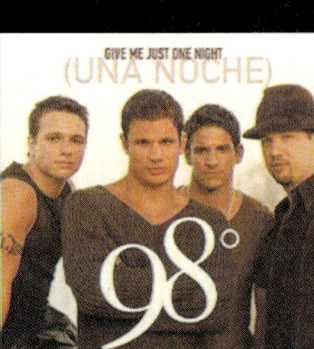

 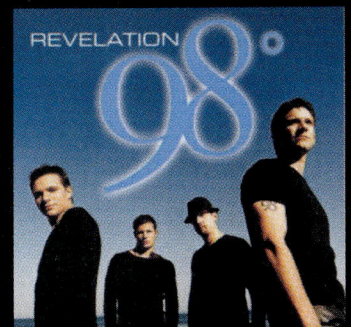  

98° ready to release hot new album and launch exciting concert tour

Jeff Timmons, Justin Jeffre and Drew and Nick Lachey realize how fickle fans can be.

Since the four members of 98° released the multi-platinum smash CD "98° And Rising," other artists such as Hanson and Third Eye Blind have watched as their new music failed to generate much radio airplay or fan interest.

Of course, artists such as *NSYNC and Backstreet Boys have had tremendous success with their new CDs, and new acts like BBMak and Westlife are breaking through as well.

So, what's in store for 98° as the group prepares to release its fourth full-length CD? All indications are that 98° could end up generating more heat than ever before!

 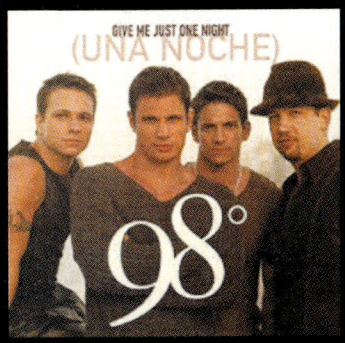 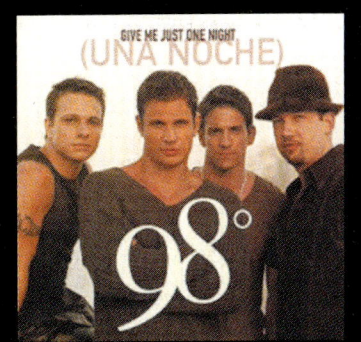 

BACK IN BUSINESS

"Revelation" is the much-anticipated follow-up CD to "98° And Rising," which has sold more than 5 million albums to date and yielded three Top 10 hit singles: "Because of You," "The Hardest Thing" and "I Do (Cherish You)." The new album is due in stores Sept. 26.

Recorded in Los Angeles and produced mainly by Anders Bagge and Arnthor Birgisson, "Revelation" not only showcases the four young men's talents as individuals, but marks their collective evolution as one of the industry's premier vocal groups.

"Revelation" packages a lot of energy, classic showmanship and passion with an exceptional array of a cappella interludes, spirited up-tempos and 98°'s unique blend of harmony-infused ballads, mostly written or co-written by the Ohio foursome.

"This next album is going to be a very, very mature album," Jeff said. "You're going to see us grow vocally as well as musically. We're going to write a lot more songs than we did on the last CD ("98° And Rising"), and we'll produce probably the majority of the album. So definitely look for us to take a step in a more mature direction as a group."

Drew added, "The new album is going to be great! A lot more up-tempos, the same quantity of ballads and mid-tempos as well."

Some fans might be surprised by the number of up-tempo songs from a group known most for its smooth, slow harmonies, but the guys say they wanted to take things in new musical directions.

"The up-tempo stuff is something that has been lacking on our previous albums," Jeff said. "Every time we go to a club with music playing in the background we never hear any of our stuff because it's too slow! So we wanted to make some music that would get people out of their seats and put that on the album."

Nick added, "We want to continue to make great music and basically expand on what we started to do already. And we want to continue to have fun in what we do. We're doing more writing and producing on this new album. We made a conscious effort to write and produce more, and we're off to a good start on that. It's definitely something we want to be involved with."

So, will the traditional, a cappella singing 98° is famous for get any space on the new CD?

"Actually we might not have any a cappella songs, but we'll definitely have some a cappella interludes," Justin said. "We've written a lot of songs for the album, and it's hard to choose the very best ones. But we're excited about what we've come up with."

For the first single off "Revelation," 98° selected the Latin-tinged "Give Me Just One Night (Una Noche)," following in the pop-music footsteps of current stars like Ricky Martin, Enrique Iglesias and Marc Anthony. Little did the guys know that their new song would break records right away!

Of 172 Top 40 radio stations that report changes to their weekly playlists, an astonishing 170 of them added "Give Me Just One Night (Una Noche)" in the first week of release. That shattered the previous record for "adds" set previously by Britney Spears' "Oops! ... I Did It Again," which was picked up by 155 stations in its first week.

MIKE KLINE/WILDSHOTS LLC (3); WALTER WEISSMAN/GLOBE PHOTOS (2)

Universal Records executives knew the song would be huge, so the company took a unique approach to marketing it, allowing fans to download the song from Web sites like MTV.com and teenmusic.com before the song could be bought in stores. That idea created a buzz that obviously helped the song succeed.

The video for "Give Me Just One Night (Una Noche)," directed by Wayne Isham at the Mayan Ruins in Mexico, is also a big success, getting a lot of play on MTV, MuchMusic and The Box.

The rest of "Revelation" will feature a variety of songs designed to showcase the rapidly maturing talents of all four members of 98º. Besides "Give Me Just One Night (Una Noche)," the album reportedly will include "Never Give Up," a song written by Justin and Jeff, and "My Everything," a song written by Nick and dedicated to his pop-star girlfriend, Jessica Simpson.

Other tracks reportedly on the new CD include:

• "Dizzy," a hip-hop song co-written by Drew that features Nick in a rapping part;
• "You Should Be Mine," a funk-dance style song;
• "Yesterday's Letter," a ballad written by Jeff and Drew;
• and an as-yet-untitled track co-written by Nick and renowned singer/songwriter Richard Marx, who also wrote a song on *NSYNC's "No Strings Attached" CD.

Regarding "Dizzy," Nick said the rap part was "a joke at first," but the few people who got a chance to listen to the section loved it, so it stayed in the song!

Asked how he thought fans would respond to the diverse styles on "Revelation," Justin said, "I think that our fans will be impressed. We definitely deliver the ballads that people expect, and they'll be impressed with the quality of the songs and the fact that we've done so much writing. It's such a well-rounded album. Each song is so different from the others ... they all fill their own special slots."

And why was the album named "Revelation" anyhow?

"We've been through so much in the past two and a half years, being on tour and recording," Nick said. "We've learned a lot and it's been a revelation for us. We think that all that is reflected on this album, hence the title 'Revelation.'"

Once "Revelation" hits stores Sept. 26, 98º will make a few public appearances, but probably will focus on rehearsals for the group's concert tour, slated to begin in November or December. The guys say they're ready to put on their best live show yet.

"Our next show is going to be much better," Justin said. "We have a lot more production — meaning pyro, dancers and other exciting things — and of course new music from the new album. It's going to be more up-tempo and a lot more fun."

One of the most important things about touring is the opportunity it gives the guys to interact with their fans, most of whom haven't seen them in a year or two.

"It's amazing to see that we have such loyal fans," Jeff said. "We're surprised and thrilled that they are so dedicated to us."

Drew added: "There's nothing more exciting than performing and getting that kind of response from the fans. That's why we're very excited to get our new record out there and get back out on the road."

Drew, Nick, Justin and Jeff are clearly excited about the new album and tour and not too concerned about looking down the road at future projects.

"We just want to thank the fans for their patience in waiting for our new record," Drew said. "We hope you enjoy it!"

98° BIOGRAPHY

Justin Jeffre

Goin' Deep
As the "bass man" for 98°, Justin helps give the group a broader musical range. But even Justin was surprised when he initially learned just how low his singing voice could be. "I was at school singing soprano and alto, and when I came back one summer they put me in the bass section," he told Pop Star! Magazine. Obviously, Justin's low-register voice has turned out to be a tremendous asset to the group.

It's Destiny
While fame and stardom may have come as a relative surprise to the other members of 98°, Justin always had an inkling that he was destined for a career in show business. "At a very early age I had this dream," he told MTV. "It was odd in the sense that I felt like it was something that was going to happen or was meant to happen. It was a gut feeling. From the seventh grade I used to pray about it. I always believed that if you really wanted something and you worked hard toward it, you could realize it." The dream, of course, has come to be. But although Justin may have appeared destined for stardom, his path to fame and fortune as a member of 98° did not come without a great deal of dedication and perseverance. Justin began formal training as early as age 11, when he auditioned for a private performing arts school at the invitation of his cousin. Justin's talents quickly became obvious when he was one of 10 chosen out of several hundred would-be performers. He chose drama as his major, but quickly changed to music after his first year – a move that helped set the stage for Justin's place in 98°. He continued to pour his heart and soul into music for the next 15 years – and just look where that's taken him!

Steady Hand
Justin is known as the "calmest" member of 98°, according the group's other three members. They say that Justin is the one band member who is the least likely to get "riled up" or to overreact. Justin, not surprisingly, agrees with the assessment. "I think that I'm a pretty laid-back guy just in general," Justin told Pop Star! "I think that there are times when you need to worry about things and times when you can't control them anyway. I personally believe that things happen for a reason." Despite Justin's sometimes reserved nature, he has come a long way from his high school and college days where, surprisingly, he was known for having a bashful demeanor. Justin attended the University of Cincinnati, where he was a history major. And, according to Justin, he would always sit silently in the back of the class. "I used to be one of the shyest people you would ever meet," Justin said. "But, as I got older I found that it's important to live life to the fullest and don't be afraid to make a fool of yourself and have fun." These days, Justin is looking less like a fool and more like a fun, carefree guy, with a singing career that would make anyone proud!

Keeping It Real
While Justin is certainly having his share of fun as 98° continues to make a splash across the globe, he is also trying to make the most of the band's universal appeal. He believes that he and the band can use their tremendous influence to help bring about positive changes on issues that are important to its members. "[My goal] is to be big enough where we can really have an impact on certain things," he said. "I always want to make a difference." With the group's tremendous success during the past several years, Justin's goal certainly seems to be within reach. In fact, he believes that the potential for the group seems to be limited only by the dreams of its members. "We truly love music," he said. "Even if we weren't as successful, and still struggling, we would do it anyway. We love to sing and love to be in the studio. Most important, we love to do performances and have people come to the shows who are enthused about what we are doing."

QUICK STATS

Birthdate: February 25, 1973
Hometown: Mt. Clemens, Michigan
Height: 5 feet 10 inches
Weight: 150 pounds
Hair/Eyes: Brown/Blue
Favorite Sports: Soccer, tennis
Favorite Color: Blue

98°
JUSTIN

LEFT: ANTHONY CUTAJAR; RIGHT: JANET MACOSKA

98° BIOGRAPHY

Drew Lachey

Drew in Charge

While 24-year-old Drew is the youngest member of 98°, he is far from the baby of the group. In fact, band members say that Drew is usually the one who keeps everyone on schedule. Whether the guys are late for a flight or are getting ready for one of their many TV appearances, Drew's the guy that will get them moving. "The guys do sort of look to me as sort of the organized one," Drew told MTV. "I like to make sure things run smoothly." But that professional side of Drew didn't begin to take shape until he began working as a camp counselor during his senior year of high school, according to his mother. "That summer he really changed and became amazingly structured," she said. "He became the one that always had the calendar and the log and the notes. That has continued into the group, where he is the administrator." So, the next time 98° hits the stage on time, you can probably thank Drew for the group's punctuality.

Drew to the Rescue

Despite being a member of one of the nation's hottest bands and possessing drop-dead gorgeous looks that have earned him admirers across the world, Drew didn't always seem destined for the life of a famous pop star. While he had always had an interest in performing through his high school years, Drew joined the Army right after graduation. He went through basic and medic training en route to becoming an emergency medical technician (EMT). Drew went on to join the Army reserves and moved to Brooklyn, N.Y., where he continued to work as an EMT. "I was content living the blue-collar life," Drew told MTV. "I went to work every day and did my job and enjoyed it. I played softball with some of the guys I worked with and had an ordinary life." And what prompted the Cincinnati, Ohio, native to move to the Big Apple? "What better place to break into the whole medical scene and to be an ambulance driver than New York. It's emergency central over there."

Prized Possessions

Although baby-faced Drew looks just as adorable with or without a baseball cap, rare is the moment that he appears in public without one – usually with the brim turned backwards. A trend or fashion statement, perhaps? Not really, Drew says. "Well, if someday I feel like doing my hair, you might see me without a baseball hat. But, for the most part, I'm just too lazy." That "laziness" has spawned quite a collection. Drew says that he now possesses well over 100 baseball caps, many of which fans get to see during the group's numerous concerts and press appearances. His hat size? He wears a $7^{1}/_{8}$ fitted cap. But Drew has another collection that's near and dear to his heart – even more so than his prized cap collection. That would be his photographs, which he takes at almost every stop on the road and features on the official 98° Web site. "I've had so many experiences, it'd be impossible to remember them all," he told Pop Star! Magazine. "So I take a lot of pictures." So many, in fact, that he's been jokingly called the group's "unofficial" photographer.

Dream Boy

While 98° appears to have a long, prosperous future ahead, Drew eventually sees a day where he will settle down and "live the American dream." "Ten years from now, I want a family, and the house with the white-picket fence and the dog," he told MTV. But don't expect Drew to fade from the music scene – with or without 98°. He hopes to continue his music career either in song writing or as a musical consultant. And while Drew would likely be a smashing success in either endeavor, don't be surprised if the success of 98° keeps him busy for a long time to come.

QUICK STATS

Birthdate: August 8, 1976

Birthplace: Cincinnati, Ohio

Height/Weight: 5'6" / 148

Hair/Eyes: Brown/Hazel

Favorite Sports: Basketball, football

Favorite Color: Navy Blue

98° DREW

98° BIOGRAPHY

Nick Lachey

Sibling Rivalry

One of the more interesting relationships among the members of 98° is the one between Nick and Drew. The two have more in common than just their membership in the quartet. As any true 98° fan knows, the two are brothers – which might help explain the dreamy good looks that they share. But although Nick is the older of the two, it was baby brother Drew who inadvertently helped push Nick into show business. A little envious of the attention Drew received from his family after Drew was accepted into a Cincinnati-area performing arts school, Nick – then 12 – decided he would audition for the school as well. "He got in and my family made such a huge deal about it and about how talented he was," Nick told MTV. "So I decided that I was going to go down there and audition too, and show these people that it wasn't such a big deal. So I did and I got in. I ended up going and fell in love with it and never left." Fortunately, the brothers' relationship has matured with age. "It's very different from what it was," Nick said. "We have always been close, but as little kids we had that typical brother rivalry. Then, when I went to college, I think we both grew up a lot and became friends more than brothers. That's the point where all the pettiness was gone."

Root, Root, Root for the Home Team

Even with all the success Nick has seen with 98°, he hasn't forgotten his roots. A big sports fan since he was a little kid, Nick still roots for his hometown teams. He says his favorite pro teams are football's Cincinnati Bengals and baseball's Cincinnati Reds. In addition, Nick is often seen wearing the black and red colors of the University of Cincinnati Bearcats. On the road, Nick can often be found watching ESPN – or any channel that carries Bengals or Reds games. As for playing sports, Nick lists football and basketball as his favorites. In fact, if he hadn't become a world-famous pop star, Nick probably would have tried to become a pro athlete. "My childhood goal was to be a football player," Nick told Pop Star! "Then, I went to a performing arts school with no sports." And the rest, as they say, is history!

Taking a Chance

Nick's decision to join 98° originally presented quite a challenge. Nick was enrolled at Miami University of Ohio (about an hour's drive outside of Cincinnati), where he was majoring in sports medicine. While he was pursuing a career related to one of his two big passions, sports, Nick received a call about an opportunity in his other main passion, music! It was Memorial Day in 1995 when one of Nick's old high school pals phoned. This friend had teamed up with another aspiring musician in Los Angeles, and the pair was trying to launch a musical group. They invited Nick to Los Angeles to join them. He was hesitant at first, but decided to take the chance to pursue the dream of making it big. Of course, it turned out to be a good choice. The other group member turned out to be Jeff Timmons, and the two formed the core of what would become 98°. "I didn't know this guy, Jeff, but then I talked to him on the phone and I heard him sing over the phone, and he heard me sing," Nick told MTV. "The more I heard from him, the more convinced I became that this was the right thing to do."

Hanging Around

As many fans have probably noticed, Nick's arm features a sun tattoo with 98° in the middle of the design. Perhaps it should be taken as a sign that the band will be sticking around for a long time to come. "I would like us to be," said Nick to MTV. "I don't think any of us have put any limit on this group at all. I think as long as we enjoy our lives and our careers, we will stick with it."

QUICK STATS

Birthdate: November 9, 1973
Hometown: Harlan, Kentucky
Height: 5 feet 10 inches
Weight: 180 pounds
Hair/Eyes: Brown/Blue
Favorite Sports: Football, basketball
Favorite Color: Red

LEFT: ANTHONY CUTAJAR; RIGHT: JANET MACOSKA

98° BIOGRAPHY

Jeff Timmons

Big Time
While Jeff attracts a lot of attention for his considerable singing skills, the 27-year-old Ohio native also makes his female fans swoon with his nearly perfect physique. At 5 feet 8 inches tall and 160 pounds, Jeff has earned a following as one of the band's most sought-after hotties! How does he keep such a fantastic body while holding such a busy schedule with 98°? "I work out a couple of times a week," he told Pop Star! Magazine. "I just do heavy weights and low reps. Lots of stretching, too, which helps keep you toned and conditioned." But Jeff's amazing good looks didn't begin with 98°. He has been popular with the girls since high school. Jeff was also quite the man on campus at Malone College, the small Canton, Ohio, school where he played football for a year. In fact, Jeff actually decided to "slim down" for his singing career. "I used to be really, really big and bulky, like 40 pounds heavier," he said. "That came from when I played football and from eating and getting in shape for that. When we signed I lost a lot of weight and got skinny. Now, I've built back up some."

A Natural
Unlike the group's other three performers, Jeff is the only member of 98° who has had no formal singing or performing training. Obviously, that hasn't slowed down Jeff's career one bit. But just how, then, did he find his way to a show-business career? "I just kind of fell into this in college," Jeff told Pop Star! "I was a junior and met up with some guys, and some girls asked us to sing for them – so we started singing and I kind of thought it sounded good." Had his singing career not taken off, Jeff's not exactly sure what he'd be doing – although he has said he would love the opportunity to work with children, perhaps as a pediatrician or child psychologist.

Family Man
Despite the gargantuan success of 98°, Jeff has not let the band's success go to his head. He insists that fame and popularity have not changed him much and that he still just wants a simple life. "Fame is cool," Jeff told MTV. "But there are some drawbacks. Like lack of time with your family. It's really tough when you don't get to see them. I guess I'm a mama's boy and a daddy's boy at the same time." But, despite the pitfalls that come with the success, Jeff is making sure to appreciate every moment. "You get to meet all kinds of people. We get to go to great places, like Southeast Asia, and see different cultures. It's definitely a wonderful thing."

Master Plan
The future looks bright for both Jeff and 98°. The band's popularity shows no signs of subsiding, and everyone is enjoying the thrill of the group's celebrity status. Nevertheless, Jeff is quick to add that he and the other members of 98° are more than up to the challenge of handling their success. "No matter how popular we're getting, we will remain grounded guys," Jeff told MTV. "It's not going to change us." And it's because of that mindset that Jeff expects 98° to stick around for a long time to come. "You never know what the future holds," he said. "I hope we can keep on being creative and hopefully get our music out there as long as we like to do it." As for Jeff's personal future, he has no plans to leave the industry, but he is looking forward to someday slowing down and caring for a big family. "I just want to have a bunch of kids (including his now nearly 2-year-old daughter, Alyssa), settle down and be happy. That's what life is all about anyway."

QUICK STATS

Birthdate: August 30, 1973
Hometown: Canton, Ohio
Height: 5 feet 8 inches
Weight: 160 pounds
Hair/Eyes: Brown/Blue
Favorite Sports: Football
Favorite Colors: Orange and Blue

98°
JEFF

98° Turns Up The Heat

Success is a 'Revelation' for this fine Ohio foursome

By David Fantle and Thomas Johnson

When red-hot musical group 98° hits the stage, fans' hearts palpitate and temperatures rise. The four-man vocal group has been generating enough heat to give other groups, like Backstreet Boys and *NSYNC, a run for their money. But do not label 98° just another "boy band."

"We formed on our own, have fans from ages four to 54, and we perform and sing live at our shows. This boy band labeling doesn't sit well with us at all," said 98° member Drew Lachey.

But that's not a direct salvo fired at Backstreet Boys or *NSYNC. In fact, 98° count the *NSYNC members as friends.

The group's official Web site – www.98degrees.com – offers this response to the "boy band" label: "It really depends on what you mean by 'boy band.' If you mean a clean cut group of young men singing pop/R&B music targeted largely to a young audience, then, yes, they can be described as a boy band and they accept that. If you mean a pre-fabricated, marginally talented group of guys who lip sync their concerts, have little or no creative input, and dance better than they sing, then no, 98° does not consider themselves a boy band."

98°'s popularity is reaching new heights with the August release of the group's first single from "Revelation," the follow-up CD to 1998's "98° and Rising." The CD reportedly will contain 10 songs, eight of them co-written by members of the group.

The single, "Una Noche" (Give Me Just One Night) will be followed by the CD's release on Sept. 26. Nick Lachey, described to Launch.com the Latin-flavored "Una Noche":

"Yeah, it's very exciting," said Nick. "We've had a lot more writing involvement in this album. Our first song is

98° Turns Up The Heat

called 'Una Noche.' It's an up-tempo dance song, which is exciting for us because we've never had that type of song out on radio before."

The Big Break

The anticipation of the latest album by millions of fans is not lost on the foursome from the Buckeye State of Ohio since success did not come overnight for them. In fact, the guys credit the well-known crooners of Boyz II Men with giving them their first big break.

It was at one of Boyz II Men's concerts that 98° caught the ear of Paris D'Jon, co-manager of R&B singer/songwriter Montell Jordan. A local radio station broadcasting from the concert had them sing a cappella on the air, and D'Jon was impressed by what he heard. The powerful music manager immediately booked the group on Jordan's tour, setting in motion enough music industry buzz to land the guys a recording contract with Motown Records.

Before there was 98° there were four boys from Ohio, three of whom attended the same high school – the School for Creative and Performing Arts (SCPA) in Cincinnati. At SCPA, the boys studied in an atmosphere reminiscent of scenes in the film "Fame."

Credit Jeff Timmons, tenor, born April 30, 1973, for setting things in motion in 1995. Jeff, a self-proclaimed sports fanatic, originally set his sights on a professional football career. However, while studying psychology at Kent State University, he attended a campus party and along with three other guys gave an impromptu performance for a group of girls. The response was so positive, Jeff scuttled his hopes for a NFL career, quit school the next day and moved to Los Angeles to pursue a music career. Never in his wildest dreams did he think he'd team up exclusively with a group of Ohio boys.

Through another SCPA alumnus, Timmons met Nick Lachey, tenor, born Nov. 9, 1973, who had been studying sports medicine at Miami University of Ohio. Nick quickly ditched school and flew to Los Angeles to meet Jeff. The two bonded, and Nick suggested they invite one of his friends, Justin Jeffre, to join them on what would become an excellent musical adventure.

Justin, bass, born Feb. 25, 1973, was another SCPA alum and had been studying history at the University of Cincinnati when the call came from Nick. He and Nick were buddies and had performed together on several occasions, including stints in a barbershop quartet and in an oldies cover band.

Nick's younger brother, Drew Lachey, baritone, born Aug. 8, 1976, was the last person to join the group, coming aboard in November 1995 after another prospective band member didn't work out. When Drew received the call, he was working as an emergency medical technician in New York City. It didn't take much persuasion from big brother Nick to get him to leave the rigors of an EMT's life behind for a chance at fame and fortune. Within two days of the call, he was on the road with Nick, learning the group's harmonies during the 3,000-mile cross-country road trip.

Pulling Together

The group rejected several names – including Just Us, Next Issue and Verse Four – before settling on 98°. The group believed the name conveyed the same feeling of heat and romance found in their music.

With all the pieces now in place, 98° began making the rounds at various talent shows and auditions. It wasn't easy in the beginning. The guys shared the same Los Angeles apartment and slept on a mattress taken from a trash heap. To make ends meet,

98° Turns Up The Heat

they also took odd jobs as deli workers, Chinese food deliverers, landscapers and nightclub bouncers at Sunset Strip clubs.

During the tough times, Jeff said his mom and dad were there to help.

"My parents helped me to follow this dream of starting this group, and they supported me at the very beginning when I had no money and absolutely no idea what I was doing," he said. "I owe them everything."

Just when prospects looked less than promising, the Boyz II Men concert and the signing by D'Jon came along. The four boys performed for the first time together at the House of Blues along with Montell Jordan in Los Angeles on Nov. 15, 1995.

On April 8, 1996, they signed their first record deal with legendary music label Motown Records.

The group's first self-titled CD came out in October 1997, but was reissued the following spring with an extra track, "Was It Something I Didn't Say," written by Diane Warren. The first big hit from the album, "Invisible Man," helped the record achieve gold status in December 1997. Although the song was a hit, 98° was still not burning up the charts.

But that was about to change with the release in October 1998 of the guys' follow-up CD, "98° and Rising." The boys played more of an overall "hands on" role, working with big-name producers and contributing to both the songwriting and producing process.

A highlight for the group was an opportunity to collaborate with Motown legend Stevie Wonder on the single "True to Your Heart," which was nominated for a Grammy and featured on Disney's "Mulan" soundtrack.

"When they sent the tape to us at home, I was almost in tears listening to it," Nick told Wall of Sound about the performance. "It was an awesome feeling to hear your voice with Stevie Wonder exchanging riffs and singing harmony parts together. It was completely unreal."

Within two months, and the help of the hit single, "Because of You," 98° earned its first platinum disc, representing sales of over 1 million copies.

Meeting The Fans

In April 1999, the popularity of the group was evident when the four heartthrobs made an appearance at a Los Angeles record store and more than 4,500 screaming fans showed up just to catch a glimpse of them. That same month, the group began a concert tour in support of their album with the all-girl group from Ireland B*Witched, the quartet behind the Celtic-flavored hit "C'est La Vie."

Touring with four young ladies – it was just another perk for 98°.

"Yeah, I guess you can call it that," Jeff told Wall of Sound. "We actually met them not too long ago when we were in England. They're cute girls, but I don't think any of them are our type."

Actually, it looks like bachelorhood is still in the cards for the four of them.

"It's hard for us to have relationships because we really can't give people the amount of time they want," Justin told Teen People. "And it's hard for us because we get lonely and want to have something that sort of feels stable and conformable."

Drew offered his own take on relationships.

"I think the number one thing to make a relationship last, as corny as it may sound, is communication. If you can't tell the person that you are with exactly what you are feeling, then you shouldn't be in that relationship," he said. "In my opinion the thing that makes a relationship exciting is that you never stop

Nick

Drew

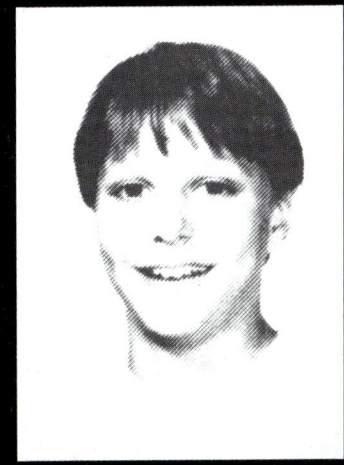
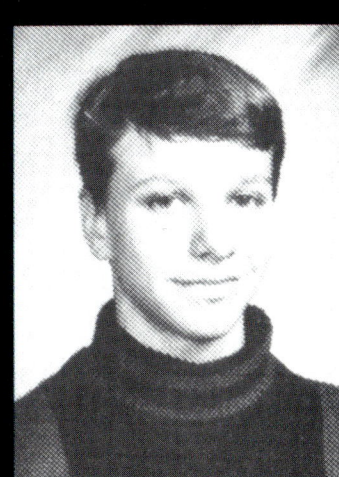

98° Turns Up The Heat

learning about the other person. I don't mean favorite colors, I mean little mannerisms. For instance, the way she looks at you in a new way from the day before or the way she cries in a movie that isn't even sad. The best things about a relationship are the little things that could easily go unnoticed."

While some of the four members of the group may be "playing the field," at least publicly, Nick has been attached to fellow songbird Jessica Simpson for several months. They met when they shared managers and then toured together. The lovebirds collaborated on a duet earlier this year, "Where You Are," for the film "Here on Earth." The two then appeared together before screenings of the film in several cities to perform the song live.

Sweetheart Jessica told Launch that the song has helped Nick shed the boy band image.

"It really separates him from all the stuff that's going on right now – all the boy band thing – because he's bigger than that, and I think with this song people will recognize that."

In October 1999, the boys decided to put some warmth into the holidays by releasing a CD of holiday chestnuts called "This Christmas." In some behind-the-scenes business dealings, the group ditched the Motown label and started recording music for Universal Records.

The band explained the movie this way: When Universal and Polygram (which owned Motown) merged in December 1998, the group decided it was a good time to move to Universal Records, which they believed had a better understanding of popular music.

The Heat Is On

"Revelation," the group's fourth album, is the much-anticipated follow-up to "98° and Rising," which has sold more than 5 million albums to date and garnered three Top 10 hit singles: "Because of You," "The Hardest Thing" and "I Do (Cherish You)." "Revelation" runs the gamut of energy, classic showmanship and keening passion with an exceptional array of a cappella interludes, spirited up-tempos and 98°'s unique blend of signature harmony-infused ballads, mostly written or co-written by the Ohio foursome.

98° recently wrapped filming a video to accompany "Give Me Just One Night (Una Noche)," with director Wayne Isham at the Mayan Ruins in Mexico. The band also was beginning rehearsals in Los Angeles for a Disney Concert special airing in October. In the meantime, fans will be able to catch their special appearances on numerous television specials, including the Teen Choice Awards (FOX), MTV's "Making Of The Video," The Miss Teen Pageant (CBS), the Arthur Ashe Kids Day Concert (CBS) and Summer Music Mania (FOX).

Word has it that 98° will begin a major concert tour in mid-January 2001 in support of "Revelation." For the guys' legions of fans, personal appearances cannot come soon enough.

Despite the screaming from fawning admirers, Justin said he hopes that music fans will take a closer look at the music from 98° rather than their pretty faces.

"I would change the opinion of those who are not very familiar with our music," he said. "Some people just think that we're just another boy band but we write our own music and I think it's deeper and more mature."

And for those who doubt the group's staying power in the music business, Drew had a message to send.

"I say, just sit back and watch," Drew said. "The more people who doubt what we can do, the more determined we are to last."

Jeff

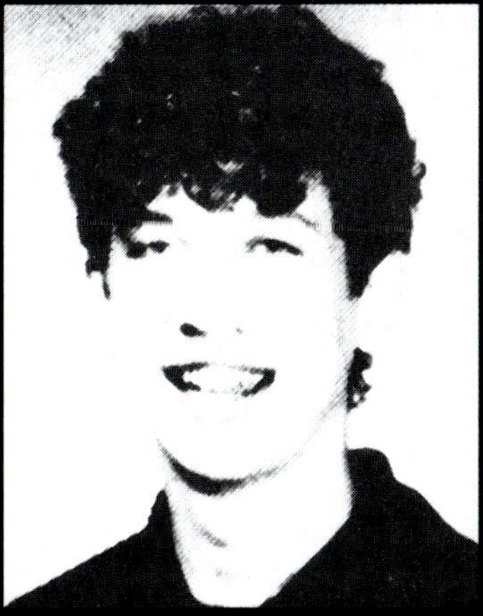

Justin

They Said It!

Drew, Nick, Jeff and Justin speak their mind!

"Nick's my best friend. He's probably going to be the best man at my wedding." – **DREW**

"Never call me Andy – it's a complete no-no. No one's ever called me that, and no one ever will." – **DREW**

"Girls overseas pride themselves on knowing every single possible fact about you. They know where I went to school – they probably know my GPA!" – **DREW**

"You would think that living together after four years and being with each other all the time we would be sick of each other. But when we have time off we still call each other and hang out together." – **DREW**

"I get to meet a lot of people, like sports idols. And that's the biggest thing for me – to meet my sports heroes. I can also get into clubs are lot more easily. There are definitely lots of advantages. It's a strange experience being a celebrity, though."
— NICK

"We're all very grounded guys. We have the proper perspective. We know as easily as fame comes, it can easily be taken away. You should enjoy it while you have it."
— JEFF

"We love doing what we're doing, and people look up to us and I hope we can inspire people. We're clean-cut and we don't get into too much trouble, but then again we're not perfect."
— JUSTIN

"For us, it's all about the fans and the music. We try to involve the audience and make them feel like a part of the show." — NICK

"I'm a really klutzy person. We did this show in Phoenix, and I was singing 'Invisible Man' and going out to the audience down these stairs. I was singing to this girl and thinking I was all cool, and on my way up I fell down on the steps!" — JEFF

"We had a good chemistry with our personalities and vocal styles. But chemistry in personalities is even more important than vocal chemistry."
— JUSTIN